INSIDE THE NFL

DALLAS COWBOYS

by Charlie Beattie

Abdo & Daughters
MIDDLE GRADE NONFICTION
An imprint of Abdo Publishing
abdobooks.com

ABDOBOOKS.COM

Published by Abdo Publishing, a division of ABDO, PO Box 398166, Minneapolis, Minnesota 55439.

Printed in China.
052025
092025

THIS BOOK CONTAINS RECYCLED MATERIALS

Cover Photos: Michael Owens/Getty Images Sport/Getty Images (Dak Prescott); George Gojkovich/ Getty Images Sport/Getty Images (Emmitt Smith)
Interior Photos: Cooper Neill/Getty Images Sport/Getty Images, 4-5, 8, 59; Matthew Pearce/Icon Sportswire/Getty Images, 6, 9, 61 (bottom right), 63; Abdo Publishing, 10-11, 58; AP Images, 12-13, 15, 20, 26, 27, 34; Focus on Sport/Getty Images, 14, 16, 19, 28, 30, 31, 43, 44, 60 (top); Vernon Biever/AP Images, 17, 18, 24-25; Bettmann/Getty Images, 21; Tony Tomsic/AP Images, 22, 23, 60 (bottom left); Paul Spinelli/AP Images, 29, 41; Focus on Sport/Getty Images Sport/Getty Images, 32, 42, 61 (top left); Wally McNamee/Corbis Historical/Getty Images, 33; Allen Dean Steele/Getty Images Sport/Getty Images, 35; Ron Heflin/AP Images, 36-37, 60 (bottom right); Tim Sharp/AP Images, 39; Greg Trott/AP Images, 45; Albert Dickson/Sporting News Archive/Getty Images, 46, 61 (bottom left); Tony Gutierrez/ AP Images, 48-49, 52; Tomasso DeRosa/AP Images, 50; Ronald Martinez/Getty Images Sport/Getty Images, 51; Kathy Willens/AP Images, 53; Ken Durden/Shutterstock Images, 54; Scott Boehm/AP Images, 55; Chris Williams/Icon Sportswire/Getty Images, 56, 61 (top right); Ron Jenkins/Getty Images Sport/Getty Images, 57

Editor: Haley Williams
Series Designer: Laura Graphenteen
Production Designer: Ryan Gale

Library of Congress Control Number: 2024948491

Publisher's Cataloging-in-Publication Data

Names: Beattie, Charlie, author.
Title: Dallas Cowboys / by Charlie Beattie
Description: Minneapolis, Minnesota: Abdo Publishing, 2026 | Series: Inside the NFL | Includes online resources and index.
Identifiers: ISBN 9781098296704 (lib. bdg.) | ISBN 9798384919223 (ebook)
Subjects: LCSH: Dallas Cowboys (Football team)--Juvenile literature. | National Football League--Juvenile literature. | Football teams--Juvenile literature. | American football--Juvenile literature.
Classification: DDC 796.33264--dc23

CONTENTS

Dallas Cowboys receiver CeeDee Lamb stretches before the team's game against the Detroit Lions on December 30, 2023.

CHAPTER 1

LEGENDARY LAMB

THE DALLAS COWBOYS HAD A JOB TO DO ENTERING WEEK 17 OF THE 2023 National Football League (NFL) season. The Cowboys needed to beat the tough Detroit Lions at home to stay alive in the race for the division title. Like the rest of his teammates, Dallas wide receiver CeeDee Lamb was focused on winning the game. But Lamb was also on the cusp of etching his name into the Cowboys' history books. And as quarterback Dak Prescott's top target, Lamb knew he would likely have to smash a record or two for his team to defeat the Lions.

Lamb entered the game with 209 catches. That put him two shy of the team's single-season record set by receiver Michael Irvin in 1995. Early in the first quarter, Dallas faced third-and-one. Lamb lined up on the right side of the field. The wide receiver sprinted up the field for 5 yards and

Lamb runs the ball during the game between the Cowboys and Lions.

then cut hard toward the sideline. As soon as he turned, Prescott's pass was there. Lamb caught it, then stopped in his tracks. A Detroit defender went sliding by, and Lamb turned up the field and weaved his way for a 31-yard gain. The catch put him one step closer to tying Irvin's record.

THE LEGACY OF 88

Many NFL teams retire the jersey numbers of great former players. That means no player from that team will ever wear the number again. Having a lot of retired numbers is often a sign that a team has a storied history.

That's not the case in Dallas, though. The Cowboys are one of the NFL's most celebrated teams. Many legends have played for "America's Team." However, the Cowboys have never officially retired a number. Instead, new players have an opportunity to prove themselves worthy of wearing a legendary number. That can come with a lot of pressure. If a young player takes the number of a former great, he must perform.

That was the pressure Lamb took on when he arrived as Dallas's top pick in the 2020 NFL Draft. Originally, he picked jersey No. 10. But he soon agreed to switch to 88 after team owner Jerry Jones mentioned wanting to see Lamb wear the number.

OUT OF CIRCULATION

Although the Cowboys don't officially retire numbers, certain jerseys worn by legendary players have not been worn in many years. No Cowboy has worn No. 74 since Hall of Fame defensive lineman Bob Lilly retired in 1974. The number 12 has not been used since quarterback Roger Staubach retired in 1980. Running back Emmitt Smith wore No. 22 and quarterback Troy Aikman wore No.8 when the Cowboys won three Super Bowls in the early 1990s. Neither number has been used since the pair left the team.

Many Cowboy greats had worn No. 88. Drew Pearson was the first to make the number famous. He was the Cowboys' top receiver during the 1970s, a decade in which Dallas won more games than any other team. In the 1980s, Irvin took on the number. He shined into the 1990s as he helped guide Dallas to three Super Bowl wins in four years. And between 2012 and 2014, wide receiver Dez Bryant wore the number for three consecutive 1,000-yard seasons.

Lamb knew what he was getting into by wearing the number. In an interview after joining the Cowboys, the young receiver said,

Retired receiver Michael Irvin, *left*, had 750 career receptions with the Cowboys.

"WHY NOT KEEP THE TRADITION GOING? OBVIOUSLY, THEY DIDN'T RETIRE THAT NUMBER FOR A REASON, SO JUST TRYING TO KEEP THE LEGACY OF 88 GOING IN DALLAS."

—CEEDEE LAMB

"Why not keep the tradition going? Obviously, they didn't retire that number for a reason, so just trying to keep the legacy of 88 going in Dallas."

With about four minutes left in the first quarter, the Cowboys trailed Detroit 3–0. Lamb remained one catch away from Irvin's record. As Irvin and other Dallas legends looked on from the sideline, Lamb knew it was go time.

GOING DEEP

On third-and-13 from the Cowboys' 8-yard line, Lamb took his spot on the right side of the field. Detroit's secondary was several yards behind the line of scrimmage to prevent a deep pass. Lamb exploded off the line and sprinted past Lions safety Kerby Joseph.

As Lamb looked for open space, the Detroit pass rush closed in on Prescott, nearly sacking him in the end zone. But Prescott escaped, rolled to his right, and searched for an open target. He spotted Lamb breaking away near midfield.

Prescott heaved a pass, and Lamb raced ahead as Joseph struggled to keep up. By the time Lamb caught the pass in stride, the Detroit safety had fallen. With no defenders in front of him, Lamb strolled down the field for a 92-yard touchdown. It was his 111th catch of the season, tying Irvin's team record.

Lamb's catch was also the second-longest reception in Cowboys history. And it was just the start of a record-smashing night. Lamb finished with 13 catches for 227 yards. In doing so, he ended the season with 1,749 receiving yards, breaking Irvin's team record. Most importantly, Lamb's performance helped Dallas pull off a tight 20–19 win. The 24-year-old receiver had already established himself as a superstar. But in a city that has always liked big and bold things from its superstars, Lamb showed throughout his record-setting season that he was worthy of his jersey number.

Lamb recorded 12 receiving touchdowns during the 2023 season.

NFL TEAMS MAP

NFC

NFC EAST

- DALLAS COWBOYS
- NEW YORK GIANTS
- PHILADELPHIA EAGLES
- WASHINGTON COMMANDERS

NFC WEST

- ARIZONA CARDINALS
- LOS ANGELES RAMS
- SAN FRANCISCO 49ERS
- SEATTLE SEAHAWKS

NFC NORTH

- CHICAGO BEARS
- DETROIT LIONS
- GREEN BAY PACKERS
- MINNESOTA VIKINGS

NFC SOUTH

- ATLANTA FALCONS
- CAROLINA PANTHERS
- NEW ORLEANS SAINTS
- TAMPA BAY BUCCANEERS

AFC

AFC EAST

- BUFFALO BILLS
- MIAMI DOLPHINS
- NEW ENGLAND PATRIOTS
- NEW YORK JETS

AFC WEST

- DENVER BRONCOS
- KANSAS CITY CHIEFS
- LAS VEGAS RAIDERS
- LOS ANGELES CHARGERS

AFC NORTH

- BALTIMORE RAVENS
- CINCINNATI BENGALS
- CLEVELAND BROWNS
- PITTSBURGH STEELERS

AFC SOUTH

- HOUSTON TEXANS
- INDIANAPOLIS COLTS
- JACKSONVILLE JAGUARS
- TENNESSEE TITANS

Cowboys head coach Tom Landry, *left*, and general manager Tex Schramm look over player names during the 1961 NFL Draft.

CHAPTER 2

DOOMSDAY

In the late 1950s, Dallas businessman Lamar Hunt wanted nothing more than an NFL expansion team in his city. But the league wasn't looking to grow. Undeterred, Hunt started his own league, the American Football League (AFL), and founded the Dallas Texans. The new league and team were set to begin play in 1960. After learning about that, the NFL owners changed their minds. Realizing they might miss out on the growing city, they granted their own expansion franchise to Dallas. The Dallas Cowboys were born.

Businessman Clint Murchison Jr. became the Cowboys' owner. He hired three men to set Dallas up for success. General manager Tex Schramm, player personnel director Gil Brandt, and head coach Tom Landry all joined the team before the first season. They would spend nearly three decades together turning the Cowboys into an iconic franchise.

Quarterback Eddie LeBaron threw a pair of touchdown passes in Dallas's first NFL victory in 1961.

Success didn't come overnight, though. In fact, the team took more than a year to record its first win. After finishing their first NFL season 0–11–1, the Cowboys finally won their opener in 1961. They then jumped out to a 3–1 start. However, the Cowboys finished the season with just four wins.

The losing continued through 1965. But Schramm and Murchison never lost faith in Brandt or Landry. Brandt's job was to identify talent, and he proved quite good at it. His standout skill was locating great players where no one else was looking. The early Cowboys featured several stars from small schools that weren't even scouted by other teams.

Once those players took the field, Landry's job was to create a winning team. The soft-spoken coach was a defensive mastermind.

Defensive tackle Bob Lilly was known as "Mr. Cowboy" because he was the first player drafted by Dallas.

As the defensive coordinator for the New York Giants in the 1950s, he had helped pioneer the 4-3 defense. The formation featured four defensive linemen and three linebackers.

With the Cowboys, Landry morphed his defense into what was called "the 4-3 Flex." Flex was short for flexible, as the defense changed from play to play depending on how the offense was lined up. With talented defensive players such as tackle Bob Lilly, end George Andrie, linebackers Lee Roy Jordan and Chuck Howley, and backs Mel Renfro and Cornell Green, few opposing offenses could get past the Cowboys. The unit was soon deemed "the Doomsday Defense."

NEXT YEAR'S CHAMPIONS

The Cowboys finally broke through in 1966. The Doomsday Defense held opponents out of the end zone, and they were matched by the NFL's best offense. Quarterback Don Meredith threw a career-high 24 touchdown passes, including a league-leading 13 to receiver "Bullet" Bob Hayes. Two years earlier, Hayes had gone to Tokyo, Japan, for the Summer Olympics and won the gold medal in the 100-meter dash. On the football field, no single player could keep up with Hayes, so teams started playing zone defense. Cowboys teammate Pettis Norman summed up Hayes's influence by saying, "Bob changed football."

Receiver "Bullet" Bob Hayes is the only person to win both a Super Bowl title and an Olympic gold medal.

The Cowboys finished the 1966 season 10–3–1 and then reached the NFL title game. But that year, a new prize was on the line. The AFL and NFL had announced a merger before the start of the season. Both leagues would come together under the NFL name in 1970. But as part of the deal, the two league champions would meet in an annual championship game starting right away in 1966. This game would later become known as the Super Bowl. The Cowboys just needed to beat the Green Bay Packers in order to move on to what is now known

Quarterback Don Meredith (17) throws a pass against the Green Bay Packers in the NFL title game on January 1, 1967.

as Super Bowl I. Playing at home in Dallas's Cotton Bowl Stadium, the Cowboys fell behind early and then spent the entire game playing catch-up. Down by seven in the final minute, Dallas faced fourth-and-goal from the Green Bay 2-yard line. Meredith rolled out but was immediately pressured by Packers defenders and threw a desperate pass. Green Bay intercepted it in the end zone to seal the 34–27 loss for Dallas.

A year later, the same two teams met in Green Bay for an NFL title-game rematch. This time, the late December temperatures

Receiver Lance Rentzel hauls in a scoring reception in "the Ice Bowl" against Green Bay in December 1967.

in Wisconsin plummeted to −13 Fahrenheit (−25° C). The game became known as "the Ice Bowl."

Once again, Dallas fell behind 14–0 in the first half. But the Cowboys battled back to 14–10 by the start of the fourth quarter. On the first play of the quarter, Dallas fullback Dan Reeves took a pitch from Meredith at the 50-yard line running left. He then stopped and lobbed a pass to wide-open receiver Lance Rentzel, who strolled in for a go-ahead touchdown.

Dallas's trick-play pass held up until the game's final seconds. But then, Green Bay drove and scored on a quarterback sneak with

13 seconds to play. Once again, the Cowboys had come up just short in a 21–17 loss.

Dallas's playoff luck didn't change for the rest of the decade. In both 1968 and 1969, the team lost divisional-round playoff games to the Cleveland Browns. The Cowboys were no longer losers, but they now had the reputation as a team that could win only in the regular season. Journalists jokingly called the team "Next Year's Champions."

Quarterback Craig Morton threw 15 touchdown passes in 1970.

BLUNDER BOWL

In 1970, the Cowboys were determined to break through. Although the offense struggled under new quarterback Craig Morton, the Doomsday Defense drove the Cowboys back to the playoffs. In what became the National Football Conference (NFC) after the merger, Dallas shut out the

Detroit Lions 5-0 in the divisional round of the playoffs. It was the lowest scoring postseason game in league history.

The Cowboys then faced the San Francisco 49ers in the NFC title game. The matchup pitted Landry against his former top defensive assistant, Dick Nolan, who was coaching the 49ers. Although Nolan had helped design the 4-3 Flex, his San Francisco offense couldn't solve it. Both Jordan and Renfro had an interception in the Cowboys' 17-10 win.

The Doomsday Defense was still at the top of its game in Super Bowl V against the Baltimore Colts. The Cowboys forced seven turnovers. But Morton threw three interceptions, and star running back Duane Thomas also lost a fumble. With 11 turnovers between the teams, Super Bowl V became known as "the Blunder Bowl." The game was tied in the final minute, but Morton's third interception set up a game-winning field goal for the Colts. Once again, Dallas came up short in a 16-13 loss.

CHUCK HOWLEY, MVP

Even though Dallas lost Super Bowl V to the Baltimore Colts, Chuck Howley turned in an excellent performance. The 34-year-old linebacker had two tackles and two interceptions. After the game, Howley was named the Super Bowl's Most Valuable Player (MVP). More than 50 years after his award, Howley was still the only Super Bowl MVP to play for the losing team.

DOOMSDAY DELIVERS

After a 4-3 start to the 1971 season, Landry had

Quarterback Roger Staubach (12) made the Pro Bowl six times during his 11 seasons with the Cowboys.

seen enough of Morton. He turned the quarterback job over to 29-year-old Roger Staubach. A former US naval officer who didn't start playing professional football until he was 27, Staubach sparked the Cowboys' offense. Dallas finished as the highest-scoring team in the NFL that year.

During the playoffs, though, the Doomsday Defense took over. In the divisional round, the Cowboys held the Minnesota Vikings to a single touchdown in the fourth quarter to help Dallas win 20–12. That was the only touchdown the Cowboys gave up that postseason.

In the NFC Championship Game on January 2, 1972, Dallas once again smothered Nolan's 49ers and won 14–3. Next up were the Miami Dolphins in Super Bowl VI. The Cowboys had another opportunity to finally win the big game.

Running back Duane Thomas, *left*, rushed for 95 yards and a touchdown in Super Bowl VI in January 1972.

The game was a defensive struggle early on. The Cowboys took advantage of a Miami fumble to build a 3–0 lead late in the first quarter. One play by the Doomsday Defense summed up the unit's punishing nature. The Dolphins faced third-and-nine from their own 38-yard line. Quarterback Bob Griese dropped back to pass. Immediately, Lilly and fellow lineman Larry Cole applied pressure. Griese kept scrambling backward in hopes of getting away. But the Dallas defensive linemen stayed right on the quarterback. Lilly finally brought Griese down at the 9-yard line.

The Doomsday Defense never let up. Howley, who had already recovered the first-quarter fumble, added an interception in the second half. In the end, the Cowboys held Miami to only 185 yards in a 24–3 victory. It was the only Super Bowl in which one team failed to score a touchdown until Super Bowl LIII in 2019.

With the victory and its first Super Bowl title, Dallas shed the label of Next Year's Champions. Although the aging defense was about to go through several changes, the Cowboys set themselves up for long-term success. Under Landry, things would only get better through the 1970s.

The Cowboys carry Landry off the field after beating the Miami Dolphins in Super Bowl VI.

Tom Landry, *right*, had a record of 250–152–6 in 29 years as the Cowboys' head coach.

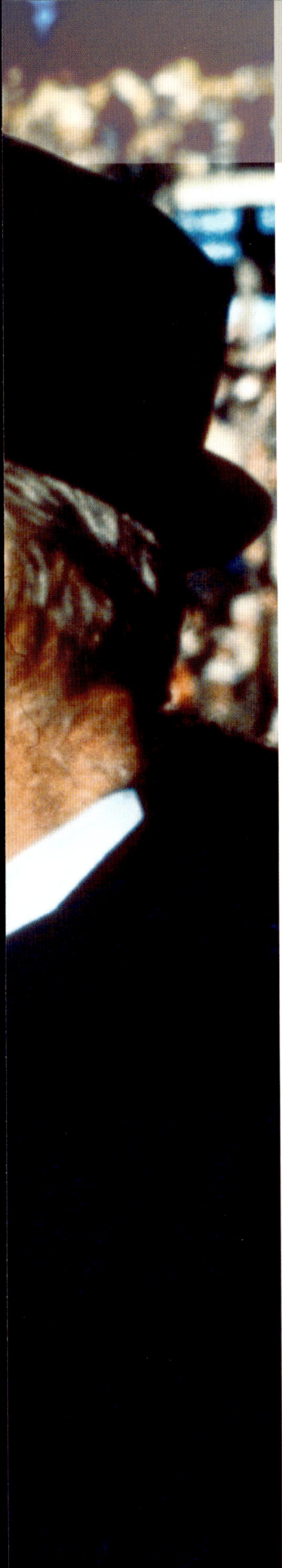

CHAPTER 3

AMERICA'S TEAM

By the mid-1970s, the Cowboys were one of professional football's most recognizable teams. And it was all part of general manager Tex Schramm's plan. Schramm helped Gil Brandt find the talent that Tom Landry molded into champions on the field. But the general manager also made sure his Cowboys were on television as much as possible.

NFL games are traditionally held on Sunday afternoons. While every Sunday-afternoon game was shown on a major network, not all games were equal. Most games kicked off at 1 p.m. Eastern time. Since so many games were on at once, local stations could show only one of them.

Schramm wanted more fans around the country to watch the Cowboys play. Since there were fewer 4 p.m. games on Sunday, they often reached a bigger audience. Schramm signed the

Cowboys up for as many late games as possible. He also worked to get the team shown on the national *Monday Night Football* game as often as he could. In addition, during the 1960s, Schramm volunteered Dallas to host an annual nationally televised game on Thanksgiving.

As a result, football fans who lived in states without professional teams got to watch the Cowboys play a lot. And since Dallas was a winning team, many people who had never even been to Texas started cheering for the Cowboys. This eventually led to Dallas becoming known as "America's Team."

THE DALLAS COWBOYS CHEERLEADERS

One of Tex Schramm's most well-known marketing ideas was creating the team's famous cheerleading squad. In the 1970s, the Dallas Cowboys Cheerleaders became national icons. The glamorous women of the team were even the subject of two movies in the late 1970s and early 1980s. The Dallas Cowboys Cheerleaders also had a reality show from 2006 to 2021 that featured contestants trying to make the squad.

The Dallas Cowboys Cheerleaders perform their famous kick line during a game in 1978.

CAPTAIN COMEBACK AND THE HAIL MARY

Fans also latched on to Dallas's popular stars, especially quarterback Roger Staubach. By 1975, Staubach had earned a reputation for late-game heroics. His ability to close out games earned him the nickname "Captain Comeback." But one play in December 1975 cemented Staubach's legacy forever.

The Cowboys trailed the Minnesota Vikings 14–10 with 32 seconds left in the divisional

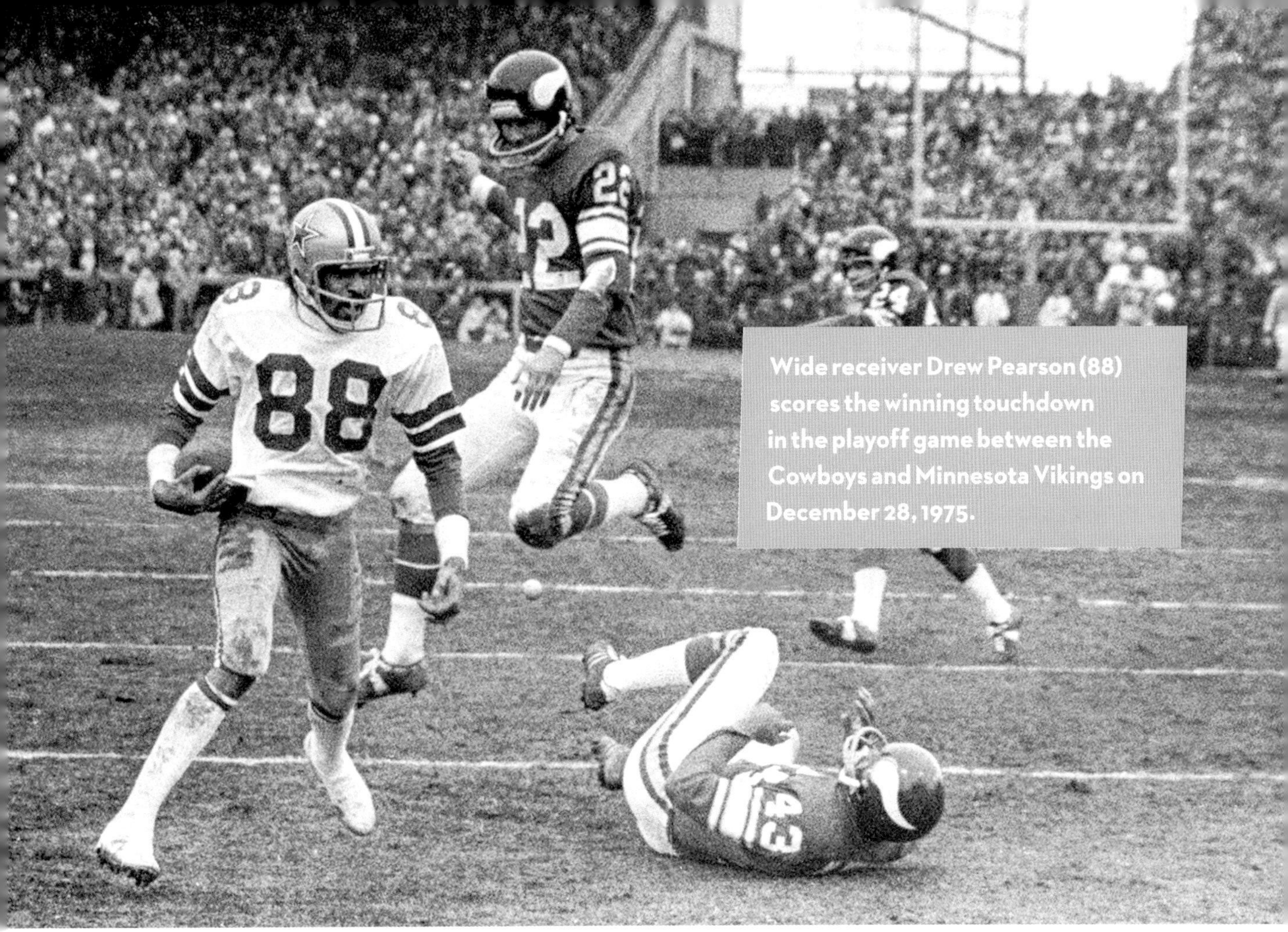

Wide receiver Drew Pearson (88) scores the winning touchdown in the playoff game between the Cowboys and Minnesota Vikings on December 28, 1975.

round of the playoffs. Stuck at the 50-yard line, the Cowboys called for a deep pass to receiver Drew Pearson. Two Vikings defenders covered Pearson as Staubach lobbed a pass his way. Pearson and Vikings cornerback Nate Wright got tangled up. Wright fell, allowing Pearson to make a basket catch at the 2-yard line and jog into the end zone for the winning touchdown.

After the game, someone asked Staubach what he was thinking when he threw the pass. A devout Catholic, Staubach replied, "I just closed my eyes and said a Hail Mary." A Hail Mary is a Christian prayer. In football, the term is used to describe a long, desperate pass that's thrown near the end zone as a last-ditch effort to score.

"I JUST CLOSED MY EYES AND SAID A HAIL MARY."

—ROGER STAUBACH

The Cowboys rode their momentum into Super Bowl X in January 1976. There, they faced the defending champion Pittsburgh Steelers. Pittsburgh led 21–10 late in the fourth quarter, but Staubach nearly pulled off another miracle. First, he threw a 34-yard scoring strike to receiver Percy Howard with 1:48 to go. The Cowboys then stuffed Pittsburgh on four plays and got the ball back at their own 39-yard line. After maneuvering his team to the Steelers' 38, Staubach tried two last-ditch heaves to the end zone. The first was incomplete, and the second was intercepted. Dallas lost 21–17.

Roger Staubach drops back to pass in Super Bowl X on January 18, 1976.

DOOMSDAY II

By 1977, the Cowboys had put together 11 winning seasons in a row. In that time, they had played in three Super Bowls and fallen one step short of the big game in four other seasons. During that stretch, many stars moved to new teams or retired. Even with a changing roster, Dallas stayed on top.

Staubach remained one of the league's top quarterbacks in 1977. And that season, he had a new star tailback to work with. Rookie Tony Dorsett was undersized at 5 feet, 11 inches, and 185 pounds, but he had a knack for finding open running lanes. Dorsett rushed for more than 1,000 yards as a rookie and added 13 total touchdowns.

Running back Tony Dorsett (33) was named the NFL's Offensive Rookie of the Year in 1977.

Dallas went through even bigger changes on defense. Several of the Doomsday Defense superstars, such as Bob Lilly, Chuck Howley, and Lee Roy Jordan, were gone. But Schramm, Brandt, and Landry replaced their veterans with young talent.

Brandt selected defensive end Harvey Martin from East Texas State in the third round of the 1973 draft. In 1977, Martin was named the NFL's Defensive Player of the Year. He played alongside Pro Bowl selection Randy White, veteran Jethro Pugh, and 6-foot-9-inch Ed "Too Tall" Jones on a fearsome defensive line. Behind them, flashy player Thomas "Hollywood" Henderson and 32-year-old D. D. Lewis anchored the linebacking spots, while Charlie Waters and Cliff Harris were both Pro Bowl–level safeties. The Cowboys held opponents to just 15.1 points per game while finishing 12–2 in 1977. The defense was nicknamed "Doomsday II."

Defensive end Harvey Martin played 11 seasons for the Cowboys from 1973 to 1983.

Dallas allowed only 13 points in playoff blowouts over the Chicago Bears and the Vikings to reach Super Bowl XII. On January 15, 1978, the Cowboys faced the Denver Broncos, whose "Orange Crush" defense was considered even better than the new Doomsday. But Dorsett got Dallas off to a good start with a 3-yard touchdown in the first quarter. Martin, White, Pugh, and Jones handled the rest. The foursome pummeled Denver's quarterbacks, with Martin recording two sacks.

By the time Staubach connected with receiver Butch Johnson on a 45-yard touchdown pass in the third quarter for a 20–3 lead, the game was effectively over. The Cowboys sealed the victory midway through the fourth when running back Robert Newhouse took a pitchout and then tossed a 29-yard score to wide receiver Golden Richards. Dallas won the championship 27–10.

The Cowboys' defense had shut down the Broncos so thoroughly that the game's MVP had to be a defensive player. But the writers couldn't decide which one. In the end, Martin and White were named co-MVPs, which had never happened before in Super Bowl history. Nearly five decades later, it hadn't happened again.

Receiver Butch Johnson, *center*, celebrates with teammates after scoring a touchdown in Super Bowl XII in January 1978.

The Cowboys and the Pittsburgh Steelers had an intense rivalry during the 1970s.

THE DROP

Dallas made it back to the Super Bowl the following season to defend its title. The Cowboys faced the Steelers on January 21, 1979. The two teams dominated their conferences in the 1970s. In Super Bowl XIII, they put on a spectacular show for football fans across the nation.

The high-scoring game featured several huge plays. In the first half alone, Staubach tossed a 39-yard touchdown, and Pittsburgh quarterback Terry Bradshaw threw touchdown passes of 28 yards and 75 yards. Dallas linebacker Mike Hegman also returned a fumble 37 yards for a touchdown.

The Cowboys trailed 21–14 with less than three minutes remaining in the third quarter. They faced third-and-three at the Pittsburgh 10-yard line. Staubach dropped back to pass

Tight end Jackie Smith's dropped pass is considered one of the biggest mistakes in Super Bowl history.

and spotted veteran Jackie Smith wide-open in the end zone. Staubach's pass flew straight to Smith's chest. But the tight end lost concentration, and the ball bounced out of his hands. Smith pounded the end zone turf in frustration while Staubach threw up his hands in disbelief. The Cowboys settled for a field goal to lower the deficit to 21–17.

Those four missed points proved to be the difference. The Steelers opened a 35–17 lead with two touchdowns 19 seconds apart in the fourth quarter. As he had three years earlier, Staubach nearly led a Super Bowl comeback. He threw a pair of touchdown passes in the final three minutes. But when Pittsburgh's Rocky Bleier recovered the Cowboys' onside kick in the final seconds, Dallas fell just short in a 35–31 loss.

DALLAS DECLINE

After the 1979 season, Staubach retired. Dallas once again had to replace a franchise icon. In 1980, longtime backup Danny White took over and immediately broke Staubach's team record for touchdown passes in a season by throwing 28. But White couldn't win over the fans, who loved Staubach's clean-cut image and thrilling comebacks. After White completed only 12 of 31 passes in a 20–7 loss to the rival Philadelphia Eagles in the NFC Championship Game, he quickly became a scapegoat for Dallas fans.

Quarterback Danny White threw 155 touchdown passes in 13 seasons with the Cowboys.

One year later, things didn't get any better for White. Once again, Dallas was back in the NFC title game, this time facing the San Francisco 49ers. With just minutes to play, White threw his second touchdown pass of the game to put Dallas up 27–21. But 49ers quarterback Joe Montana drove his team down the field and beat Dallas with a last-minute, 6-yard touchdown pass to a leaping Dwight Clark. The play became known as "the Catch" and helped launch the 49ers into a dynasty while keeping Landry's team out of the Super Bowl once again.

The 1982 Cowboys made it back to the NFC title game. This time, they took on their heated rivals from Washington. The two teams had despised each other since Dallas entered the league two decades earlier. Their matchups were often very physical. After White was knocked from the game with a concussion, backup quarterback Gary Hogeboom tried to rally the Cowboys from a 21–10 deficit in the second half. In the end, though, Dallas came up short again, losing 31–17.

Cornerback Everson Walls led the NFL in interceptions three times during the 1980s.

The aging Cowboys hung on for three more years, even winning a division title in 1985. But they couldn't get past the divisional round of the playoffs. Then in 1986, Dallas finished with a 7-9 record. That marked the team's first non-winning season since 1965, which ended the longest streak in NFL history. But soon the Cowboys would gain several stars to help turn things around.

Jerry Jones bought the Cowboys for $150 million in 1989. By 2024, the team was valued at about $11 billion.

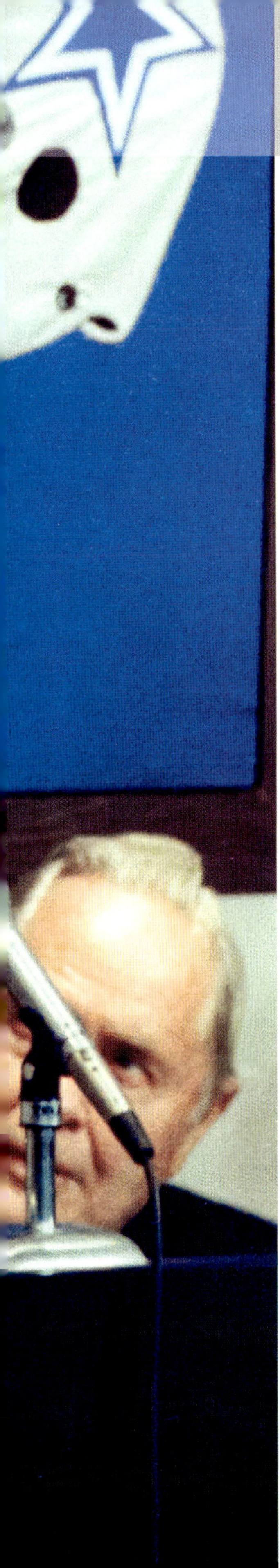

CHAPTER 4

HOW 'BOUT THEM COWBOYS

In 1988, Tex Schramm and Gil Brandt made their final first-round draft pick for the Cowboys. They selected brash wide receiver Michael Irvin from the University of Miami. The iconic Cowboys executives were both gone after that season, but Irvin would soon play a key role in the team's turnaround.

In February 1989, Jerry Jones purchased the Cowboys. A former college football player at Arkansas, Jones became a millionaire in the oil business. The new owner had big dreams for the Cowboys. However, those dreams didn't involve the old guard. As a result, Schramm left the Cowboys, and Brandt and coach Tom Landry were fired. Jones wanted to run the team front office himself, so he hired an old college teammate, Jimmy Johnson, as his head coach.

BIG PAYDAYS

Soon after Jerry Jones bought the Cowboys in 1989, he negotiated huge sponsorship deals with big companies such as Nike and Pepsi. However, Jones's deals were against NFL rules that said no team could sign deals with its own sponsors. After several lawsuits, Jones was allowed to keep his deals. And other owners soon copied his strategy. Jones's ideas are often seen as one of the biggest reasons the NFL is the richest sports league in the United States today.

Johnson couldn't have been more different from Landry. Landry was a quiet man who walked the sideline in a suit and a fedora. Johnson was talkative, wore Dallas Cowboys apparel, and never covered his perfectly styled hair.

Despite the changes, the team stumbled to a 1–15 record in 1989. Midway through the year, Dallas pulled off the biggest trade in NFL history. The team sent star running back Herschel Walker to the Minnesota Vikings along with four draft picks. Dallas received four players and eight picks in return, including Minnesota's top selections in 1990, 1991, and 1992.

At the time, the Cowboys were ridiculed for the deal, but Jones and Johnson used those picks to build a dynasty. Over the next few seasons, the Cowboys drafted stars such as defensive tackle Russell Maryland and safety Darren Woodson. But the biggest draft pick was a running back to replace Walker.

The Cowboys selected running back Emmitt Smith 17th overall in 1990. While many people thought he didn't have the speed for the NFL, Smith proved them wrong. With his huge legs churning, Smith ate up yards at a record pace. By 1991, he had worked with Irvin and young quarterback Troy Aikman to get Dallas back to the playoffs. The press dubbed them "the Triplets."

Quarterback Troy Aikman, *left*, running back Emmitt Smith, *center*, and Michael Irvin, *right*, combined for 19 Pro Bowl appearances with the Cowboys.

SUPER ROUT

The 1991 Cowboys lost in the wild-card round of the playoffs. But Dallas returned in 1992 with big expectations. The team dominated on both sides of the ball and finished 13–3. Smith led the NFL with 1,713 rushing yards and 18 rushing touchdowns. In one game against the Seattle Seahawks, the once-again dominant Cowboys' defense allowed only 62 yards in a 27–0 shutout.

After routing the Philadelphia Eagles in the divisional round of the playoffs, the Cowboys traveled to San Francisco to face the 49ers in the NFC title game. Since the 49ers had beaten Dallas in the postseason 12 years earlier, they had become one of the top teams in the NFC and had won four Super Bowls. But Dallas was able to pull off a 30–20 win thanks to a rushing and a receiving touchdown from Smith. The victory set up a new rivalry between the teams and sent the Cowboys back to the Super Bowl. In the locker room after the game, Johnson gave a fired-up speech to his team. He finished it by shouting, "How 'bout them Cowboys!"

"HOW 'BOUT THEM COWBOYS!"

—JIMMY JOHNSON

In Super Bowl XXVII, Dallas took on the high-powered Buffalo Bills. Dallas's defense made three big first-half plays. In the first quarter, defensive end Charles Haley pressured Buffalo quarterback Jim Kelly inside the Bills' 10-yard line. Kelly fumbled after Haley's hit, and Dallas defensive lineman Jimmie Jones recovered the ball and scored a touchdown. Then in the second quarter, Buffalo had fourth-and-goal at the Dallas 1-yard line when Cowboys safety Thomas Everett intercepted Kelly in the end zone.

The Cowboys went up 21–10 with 1:54 left in the half on an 18-yard touchdown pass from Aikman to Irvin. Then Dallas recovered another fumble at the Bills' 18. One play later, Aikman rifled a pass to Irvin along the right sideline at the 2-yard line. Irvin made a leaping catch, then spun and avoided a defender as he dove into the end zone.

The Cowboys didn't let up in the second half. In one of the biggest blowouts in Super Bowl history, the Cowboys routed Buffalo 52–17. In just four years, Jerry Jones, Johnson, and the Triplets had taken the Cowboys from the worst team in the NFL to the best.

Aikman (8) was named the MVP of Super Bowl XXVII in January 1993 after throwing for 273 yards and four touchdowns.

SHOULDERING THE LOAD

The defending Super Bowl champions got off to a rough start in 1993. With Smith sitting out as he negotiated a bigger contract, Dallas lost its first two games. Once Smith got his new deal and returned to the field, the rest of the NFL paid the price. Running behind a powerful offensive, Smith led the league in rushing yards even with the missed time.

Dallas needed to win its final game on the road against the New York Giants to secure home-field advantage in the playoffs. But late in the second quarter, Smith separated his shoulder after slamming hard into the turf. That kind of injury usually knocked players out of action. Despite the injury causing Smith intense pain, he played on. He tallied 168 yards on 32 carries and caught 10 passes for

61 yards. Dallas won the key game 16–13, and Smith earned the NFL's MVP Award.

The win meant the NFC Championship Game between the Cowboys and 49ers was played in Dallas. Smith delivered with 88 rushing yards, 85 receiving yards, and two touchdowns. The Cowboys won 38–21.

Smith rushed for 289 yards in three Super Bowl appearances with the Cowboys.

Once again, Dallas faced the Bills in the Super Bowl. This time, the game was tied 13–13 early in the third quarter. Dallas took over at its own 36-yard line. Smith carried the ball seven times on an eight-play drive. On his final carry, the superstar back slipped a tackle in the backfield and burst through a hole for a 15-yard touchdown. Behind Smith's 132 yards and two touchdowns on 30 carries, the Cowboys pulled

Smith, *left*, recorded more than 1,000 rushing yards in 11 of his 13 seasons with the Cowboys.

away to win 30–13. And Smith walked away with the Super Bowl MVP Award.

PICKING A WINNER

After winning Super Bowl XXVIII, everything seemed perfect in Dallas. The Cowboys had won back-to-back titles. They had glitzy superstars at seemingly every position. Cowboys fans were back to loving "America's Team," while jealous rivals hoped Dallas would finally lose.

However, behind the scenes, Jones and Johnson were having problems getting along. The two old friends struggled over

Jimmy Johnson, *left*, had a 44–36 record in five seasons as Dallas's head coach.

who should get the most credit for the team's success. The issue became so heated that Jones shockingly let Johnson go before the 1994 season.

Under new head coach Barry Switzer, the Cowboys fell short of the Super Bowl when they lost to the 49ers in the NFC title game. Jones hated losing and wanted to do everything he could to get back to the top. Early in the 1995 season, he turned heads by signing superstar cornerback Deion Sanders from the 49ers to a huge seven-year, $25 million contract.

Cornerback Deion Sanders, *in white*, intercepted 14 passes with the Cowboys from 1995 to 1999.

Nicknamed "Prime Time" for his flashy moves on the field, Sanders was one of the best cornerbacks to ever play in the NFL. Opposing quarterbacks were so afraid of Sanders intercepting the ball that they rarely dared to throw it to the

Cornerback Larry Brown races downfield after one of his two interceptions in Super Bowl XXX on January 28, 1996.

player he was covering. Sanders had good enough hands that the Cowboys also used him on offense.

The Cowboys finished the 1995 regular season with a 12–4 record. They then beat the Eagles and Green Bay Packers in the playoffs to get back to the Super Bowl. There, they faced the Pittsburgh Steelers, their old Super Bowl rivals from the 1970s.

Sure enough, Steelers quarterback Neil O'Donnell barely tested Sanders. But in the second half, a different Cowboys defensive player burned O'Donnell. With 7:42 left in the third quarter and Dallas up 13–7, O'Donnell overshot his receiver and threw the ball right to Dallas cornerback Larry Brown, who raced 33 yards to the Pittsburgh 18. After Aikman hit Irvin on a 17-yard pass, Smith punched the ball in from the 1-yard line to put Dallas up 20–7.

Pittsburgh lowered the deficit to 20–17 with just over seven minutes to play. Once again, O'Donnell tested Brown, who cut in front of a receiver and intercepted the ball at the Pittsburgh 39. This time, Brown took off down the sideline and was forced out of bounds at the 6-yard line. Two plays later, Smith scored on a 4-yard run to seal a 27–17 victory. On a Cowboys team filled with several future Hall of Famers, Brown was named one of the most unlikely Super Bowl MVPs ever.

The Cowboys had become the first NFL team to win three Super Bowls in four seasons. And in a span of seven years, Jones had become one of the NFL's most powerful owners. However, a dynasty that looked as if it would last for several more years soon came crashing down.

Emmitt Smith recorded a league-record 164 rushing touchdowns during his NFL career.

CHAPTER 5

FIGHTING TO GET BACK

IN THE LATE 1990S, THE TEAM THAT HAD ONCE RULED THE LEAGUE slowly came apart. The Cowboys were no longer the best in the NFL. Team owner Jerry Jones tried everything to stay on top, from firing coaches to handing out big free-agent paychecks. But nothing worked. The team made three playoff appearances between 1996 and 1999 but didn't make it past the divisional round. Then Michael Irvin retired in 1999, and Troy Aikman followed a year later. This left Emmitt Smith as the last of the Triplets on the team.

In 2002, the Cowboys were on their way to a third straight 5–11 season. Fans still had a reason to show up at Texas Stadium on Sundays, though. Smith was chasing the NFL's all-time rushing mark. In Week 8 against the Seattle Seahawks, Smith took a handoff and burst through a hole on the left side. Although he stumbled, he managed to keep his balance and lunge for 11 yards. The play gave him 16,727 career rushing yards, breaking former Chicago Bears legend Walter Payton's record. The game was stopped for several minutes as former teammates came onto the field to honor Smith.

Led by All-Pro safety Roy Williams, the Cowboys held opponents to just 16.4 points per game in 2003.

DIAMOND IN THE ROUGH

Smith left Dallas before the 2003 season. That year also marked the beginning of a new era under a high-profile head coach. Jones hired Bill Parcells, who had led the New York Giants to two Super Bowl victories. The legendary coach led a big turnaround, pushing the Cowboys to a 10–6 record with one of the best defenses in the league. But the Cowboys were blown out 29–10 by the Carolina Panthers in the wild-card round of the playoffs. It was the final game in a Dallas uniform for beloved safety Darren Woodson, one of the last on-field links to the team's glory years.

Safety Darren Woodson (28) retired as the Cowboys' all-time tackles leader with 1,350.

In trying to get Dallas back to the top, Jones continued to spend money on big-name free agents. Then in 2006, the Cowboys found their next star in an unlikely place. Quarterback Tony Romo had signed with Dallas as an undrafted free agent in 2003 out of Eastern Illinois. The team nearly cut him before his rookie season, and he only saw playing time as a kick holder during his first two seasons. But when starter Drew Bledsoe struggled against the Giants in Week 7 of the 2006 season, Romo came on in relief. The unheralded quarterback threw two touchdown passes. Although Dallas lost the game, Romo impressed Parcells and became the Cowboys' new starter. Romo led the Cowboys to six wins in their last 10 games to help them reach the playoffs.

In the wild-card round, Dallas trailed the Seahawks 21–20 with less than five minutes remaining. Romo guided Dallas inside the Seattle 5-yard line with 1:19 left before the Cowboys were forced into a field-goal attempt. Romo bobbled the snap but scooped up the ball and tried to race around the left end for a touchdown. However, a Seattle defender clipped Romo's ankles just before he could reach the goal line, and he fumbled the ball as he landed. The Cowboys couldn't get the ball back in time to score again and suffered a heartbreaking loss.

Quarterback Tony Romo had a team-record 34,183 passing yards with the Cowboys.

One year later, Romo tossed a team-record 36 touchdown passes as he formed a strong connection with tight end Jason Witten and wide receiver Terrell Owens. The Cowboys won 13 games for their best record since 1992. But once again, the team came up short in the playoffs. Despite being heavily favored against the visiting Giants, Dallas fell 21–17.

NO CATCH

Romo continued to smash team records as he put together strong seasons. But the Cowboys struggled to succeed in the playoffs. After the 2009 regular season, they finally broke their 13-year postseason losing streak by routing the Philadelphia Eagles 34–14 in the wild-card round. But a week later, Dallas was crushed 34–3 by the Minnesota Vikings.

Tight end Jason Witten (82) was named to the Pro Bowl 11 times in 16 seasons with the Cowboys.

The Cowboys didn't return to the playoffs until the 2014 season. Romo, by then the team's all-time leading passer, had a new top weapon in receiver Dez Bryant. The passionate fifth-year player led the NFL with 16 touchdown catches as Dallas won the NFC East. Romo then led a comeback in the wild-card round to beat the Detroit Lions 24–20.

On the road in Green Bay for the divisional round, the Cowboys trailed the Packers 26–21 with less than five minutes remaining. On fourth-and-two from the Green Bay 32-yard line, Romo lobbed a pass down the left sideline for Bryant. The 6-foot-2-inch receiver made a leaping catch at the 5-yard line then came down and made two stumbling steps. Instantly, Cowboys fans were reminded of Drew Pearson's game-winning playoff catch in 1975. Bryant was even wearing No. 88, just as Pearson had been. As Bryant fell in the end zone, though, he juggled the ball before securing it.

Bryant's play was initially ruled a catch. But the Packers challenged the ruling. After a replay review, the officials said that Bryant didn't have control of the ball all the way to the ground. The Packers took over, and Dallas never got the ball back.

The controversy over Bryant's no-catch was one of the biggest debates in football. It led to the NFL changing its catch rule in 2017. The new rule stated that if a player catches the ball and makes a football move, such as taking additional steps, he doesn't have to keep control once he hits the ground. Under the new rule, Bryant's play would have been a catch. But that didn't help the Cowboys against Green Bay, and they lost 26–21.

JERRY WORLD

In 2009, the Cowboys built a brand-new stadium. In true Texas fashion, it was both huge and glamorous. AT&T Stadium officially holds 80,000 fans, but it can fit more than 100,000 when standing-room tickets are sold. It also features a 160-foot (49 m) long scoreboard over the field. The stadium, which cost $1.15 billion to build, is often referred to as "Jerry World," after team owner Jerry Jones.

DAK ATTACK

In 2016, a back injury knocked Romo out of the lineup. To replace him, the Cowboys

Receiver Dez Bryant (88) leaps for a pass in the playoff game against the Packers in January 2015. The pass was controversially ruled incomplete.

found a new young star at quarterback. The team had picked Dak Prescott in the fourth round of that year's draft. Not many expected the former Mississippi State player to be an NFL star. But the rookie stepped in and threw 23 touchdown passes and only four interceptions as he led Dallas back to the postseason. Head coach Jason Garrett stuck with Prescott even after Romo returned.

In 2021, quarterback Dak Prescott broke the Cowboys' single-season record for touchdown passes by throwing 37.

In the divisional round of the playoffs against Green Bay, Prescott threw three touchdown passes, including two to Bryant. Rookie running back Ezekiel Elliott, who finished second to Prescott in the NFL's Rookie of the Year voting, added 125 rushing yards. But with 1:33 left in the game, the Cowboys trailed by three. In less than one minute, Prescott led the team down the field to set up a 51-yard field goal from kicker Dan Bailey. That tied the game 31–31.

However, the Packers got the ball back and completed a 36-yard pass on third-and-20 with 12 seconds to go. The Packers then kicked a 51-yard field goal to beat the Cowboys 34–31.

During the following seasons, Dallas didn't see a ton of success. But Prescott eventually took the field with the team's newest generation of stars. Receiver CeeDee Lamb was the Cowboys' top draft pick in 2020. Donning the team's iconic No. 88 jersey, he soon began smashing records. Then in 2021, pass-rushing linebacker Micah Parsons won the NFL's Defensive Rookie of the Year Award.

Despite their new talent, the Cowboys continued to struggle in the playoffs. Between 2021 and 2023, Dallas won 12 games each season and entered the postseason with high hopes, but the

Linebacker Micah Parsons (11) recorded 12 or more sacks in each of his first four seasons with the Cowboys.

COWBOYS TROPHY CASE

SUPER BOWL CHAMPIONSHIPS: 5

Super Bowl VI – January 16, 1972
Super Bowl XII – January 15, 1978
Super Bowl XXVII – January 31, 1993
Super Bowl XXVIII – January 30, 1994
Super Bowl XXX – January 28, 1996

CONFERENCE CHAMPIONSHIPS: 8

1970, 1971, 1975, 1977, 1978, 1992, 1993, 1995

DIVISION TITLES: 26

NFL East: 1966
NFL Capitol: 1967, 1968, 1969
NFC East: 1970, 1971, 1973, 1976, 1977, 1978, 1979 1981, 1985, 1992, 1993, 1994, 1995, 1996, 1998, 2007, 2009, 2014, 2016, 2018, 2021, 2023

All stats are through the 2024 season.

Prescott (4) started in eight games in 2024 before an injury in Week 9 ended his season.

team never got past the divisional round. In 2024, the Cowboys suffered numerous injuries and won only seven games, missing the playoffs entirely.

Fans around the nation who loved the team were left frustrated and wondering when Dallas would finally get back on top. Meanwhile, anyone rooting against the Cowboys celebrated their failures. But as one of the most popular sports teams in the country, Dallas continued getting plenty of media attention. Win or lose, Cowboys fans had hope in "America's Team."

TIMELINE

1960 The Cowboys finish 0-11-1 in their first season.

1966 Dallas finishes with its first winning record but falls in the playoffs.

1967 The Cowboys lose "the Ice Bowl" on December 31 to finish as the NFL's runner-up for the second straight year.

1972 Dallas wins its first Super Bowl by dominating the Miami Dolphins 24-3 on January 16.

1978 Dallas shuts down the Denver Broncos to win Super Bowl XII on January 15.

1989 Jerry Jones buys the Cowboys and fires legendary coach Tom Landry.

1993 On January 31, the Cowboys beat the Buffalo Bills 52-17 in Super Bowl XXVII.

Emmitt Smith is named Super Bowl MVP as Dallas repeats as champion on January 30.

1994

Smith becomes the NFL's all-time rushing leader in his final season with the Cowboys.

2002

Quarterback Dak Prescott is named the NFL Offensive Rookie of the Year.

2016

1996

Led by Larry Brown's two interceptions, Dallas beats the Pittsburgh Steelers in Super Bowl XXX on January 28.

2006

Tony Romo makes his first start at quarterback on his way to becoming Dallas's all-time leading passer.

2023

Receiver CeeDee Lamb breaks the Dallas record for catches in a season.

GLOSSARY

backfield–the area on the field behind the line of scrimmage where the offensive players line up.

concussion–a brain injury caused by a blow to the head or a violent shaking of the head and body.

contract–an agreement to play for a certain team.

draft–a system that allows teams to acquire new players coming into the league.

dynasty–a team that has an extended period of success, usually winning multiple championships in the process.

era–a period of time in history.

expansion team–a new team that is added to an existing league.

franchise–an entire sports organization.

free agent–a player who is not signed to a team.

iconic–well known for excellence.

legacy–something of importance that came from someone in the past.

merger–joining one thing with another to create something new, such as a company, a team, or a league.

pitchout–a sideways pass thrown between two backs behind the line of scrimmage.

Pro Bowl–a postseason competition that the NFL's all-stars are invited to compete in.

quarterback sneak–a play in which the quarterback takes the snap and then immediately runs or dives forward while the offensive line also moves forward.

rival–an opponent with whom a player or team has a fierce and ongoing competition.

rookie–a professional athlete in his or her first year of competition.

roster–a list of players who make up a team.

scapegoat–a person who is blamed for something bad that has happened, even if they aren't at fault.

standing-room tickets–tickets to an event that do not include an assigned seat.

veteran–someone who has played for many years.

ONLINE RESOURCES

Booklinks
NONFICTION NETWORK
FREE! ONLINE NONFICTION RESOURCES

To learn more about the Dallas Cowboys, please visit **abdobooklinks.com** or scan this QR code. These links are routinely monitored and updated to provide the most current information available.

INDEX